Whales for Kids

By Tom Wolpert

PRESS, INC

Minnetonka, Minnesota

Cowles Creative Publishing, Inc.
5900 Green Oak Drive
Minnetonka, Minnesota 55343
1-800-328-3895

Designed by Origins Design, Inc.

The **National Wildlife Federation**® is the nation's largest conservation education and advocacy organization.
Since 1936, NWF has educated people from all walks of life to protect nature, wildlife and the world we all share.

Ranger Rick® is an exciting magazine published monthly by National Wildlife Federation®, about wildlife, nature,
and the environment for kids ages 7 to 12. For more information about how to subscribe to this magazine, write or call:
Ranger Rick Department, National Wildlife Federation, 8925 Leesburg Pike, Vienna, Virginia 22184, 1-800-588-1650.

©National Wildlife Federation, 1997 ™ and ® designate trademarks of
National Wildlife Federation and are used, under license, by NorthWord Press, Inc.

Library of Congress Cataloging-in-Publication Data

Wolpert, Tom 1947-
    Whales for kids / by Tom Wolpert.
        p. cm.
    Includes index.
    Summary: Discusses the physical characteristics and behavior of the
    largest animal that ever lived.
        ISBN 1-55971-475-1
    1. Whales—Juvenile literature. (1. Whales.) I. Title.
    QL737.C4W66   1990
    599.95—dc20   91-16177
                                            CIP
                                            AC

Printed in Malaysia

Whales swim the oceans of the world. They dive to great depths and cruise the sunny waves as they please. That's because they are the largest animals that ever lived.

The blue whale, for instance, may grow 90 feet long and weigh 300,000 pounds. In fact, a dinosaur, an elephant and a man could fit on a blue whale's back with room to spare.

Whales may look like fish, but they are not fish at all. Whales are *mammals* — just like dogs, cats, cows and human beings.

Because they are mammals, whales give birth to live young (fish lay eggs). Baby whales nurse on their mother's milk (young fish do not nurse at all). Whales breathe through lungs and must hold their breath (fish breathe through gills).

But whales are also very different from most mammals. For example, compare yourself to a whale. You can smell with your nose (a whale has no sense of smell). You hear with ears (a whale can hear but has no real ears — only tiny ear openings). You have four limbs — two legs and two arms (a whale has only two front limbs called *flippers*). So, even though humans and whales are both mammals, they are very different from one another.

Some types of whales feed and travel in groups which sometimes number hundreds of whales. These large groups are called herds or pods. Other whales travel in small family groups of two or three animals. A family group may include a bull (adult male); a cow (adult female); and a calf (a baby or immature whale).

Female whales carry their young inside their bodies for up to eighteen months before giving birth. When born, calves do not have enough *blubber* to float. Mother whales keep their calves in constant motion to help them breathe.

After one month, the calves have developed enough blubber to float and swim without help. They now spend most of their time playing and learning to turn, roll, dive and touch. Sometimes when a calf becomes too playful the mother hugs it against her stomach with her flippers until the calf calms down.

Whales swim by thrusting their powerful tail fins up and down. These fins are called *flukes*. Their flippers are used only for balance and turning. Most whales swim at a speed of three to five miles per hour. However, blue and killer whales can go as fast as 25 miles per hour!

Adult whales will use their size and power to protect their young. Whales have only one enemy other than man. That enemy is the killer whale. Whales do not, as far as we know, fight among themselves, and whales seldom attack boats unless they have been wounded.

Whales swim and dive most of the time. To protect their eyes from the salty ocean water, the whales produce an oily substance that covers them. Whales depend on their sense of hearing more than their sense of sight. Sound travels faster through the water than through air, and this is important to whales since they have excellent hearing. Whales do not sleep for long periods of time but take naps for a few minutes at a time at the surface of the water.

Even though whales breathe air, they would die on land. If a whale is stranded on land, the great weight of its body presses down on its lungs and the whale will *suffocate*. It needs the water to support its huge body.

As you can guess, whales have pretty big appetites. Larger whales eat nearly a ton of food daily. When whales dive for food, the air in their lungs becomes hot and moist from body heat. Upon reaching the surface, they blow the air out through a hole in the top of their head. The hot breath strikes the cold air outside and *condenses* to form a spout of fog.

These fog spouts, or "blows", alert people to the presence of whales from great distances. Most people wish only to observe the gentle, even friendly, whales. Others, however, are commercial hunters who kill whales for their meat, hide and body oil.

Some whales were once hunted nearly to *extinction*. Fortunately, the majority of people and their governments today wish to save and protect whales throughout the world. Someday the whales may cruise the sunny waves without harm from humans at all. That will be good news for whales and whale-lovers like you and me.

The *origins* of the whale date back about sixty million years (60,000,000) to members of a family of early mammals known as *mesonychids*. Mesonychids were some of nature's earliest designs for life on earth. They had four legs and a tail. They were furry, carried their babies inside their bodies until birth and nursed their young.

Some of these early mammals lived along the shores of swamps and *estuaries*. They probably walked along the beaches searching for food.

Eventually, some began wading in the water in search of food. They would hold their breath to duck their heads under the water to gather food. As they waded deeper, they found more food. Soon some began to dive and swim in the shallows.

The longer they stayed at sea the better they fared. The sea provided a plentiful supply of food. Over a long period of time they found that all their needs could be met in the sea. They had no reason to return to land. These land mammals evolved, over thousands of years, into sea animals. They *adapted* to a new environment.

Once at sea they gradually took the shape of fish. Today, whales are so well adapted to life underwater that it is easy to forget they were once mammals of the land. Remember, this change from land life to sea life took place thousands of years ago.

Not all mesonychids became sea mammals. Many survived well with the food available on land. In time these mammals evolved into modern *artiodactyls*. We know this kind of animal as the antelope, buffalo, caribou, cow, pig, moose, and musk-ox.

Probably the land mammal that is most closely related to the whale is the hippopotamus. It is surprising to think of the whale and hippopotamus as being related, but they are.

The Toothed Whales

Toothed whales eat fish and squids. Although they can hold their prey in their peg-like teeth, they swallow their food whole without chewing it. A sperm whale could easily swallow a man.

Sperm Whale:
Maximum length - 65 feet
Weight - 60 tons (120,000 lbs.)

Characteristics: The sperm whale is the largest toothed whale. It has 35 to 65 teeth. Its enormous head makes up a third of the body length. The head contains an enormous amount of "spermaceti" a waxy material used in cosmetics. This is one reason it is still hunted and killed. A sperm whale is dark gray and may be found in all oceans.

Narwhal Whale:
Maximum length - 18 feet
Weight - 2 tons (4,000 lbs.)

Characteristics: The male narwhal whale has a spiral ivory tusk about eight feet long jutting from the left side of its head. The female narwhal has no tusk. The narwhal is gray-white with dark gray or black spots on its skin and is found in arctic regions.

Bottlenose Whale:

Maximum length - 30 feet
Weight - 30 tons (60,000 lbs.)

Characteristics: The bottlenose whale has four teeth. Its forehead has a distinctive swelling. The bottlenose whale is dark in color and lives in the North Atlantic and Antarctic regions.

Giant Bottlenose Whale:

Maximum length - 42 feet
Weight - 30 tons (60,000 lbs.)

Characteristics: The giant bottlenose whale has four teeth. Its snout narrows into a round "beak," like the neck of a bottle. The giant bottlenose whale is black or dark gray in color and lives in the north Pacific and Antarctic regions.

Killer Whale :

Maximum length - 30 feet
Weight - 10 tons (20,000 lbs.)

Characteristics: The killer whale has a glossy black back and a
white underside. It has 40-48 teeth – ten to twelve teeth on each

side, upper and lower, on each jaw. Killer whales travel in groups of two to dozens and can travel up to 25 miles per hour. They primarily eat salmon and other large fish. However, they sometimes attack porpoises, seals, walruses, and newborn whales. Killer whales are found in all oceans but especially in cold regions.

The Baleen Whales

Baleen whales are toothless. They eat *plankton,* a mixture of small sea animals and plants. When a baleen whale approaches, a mass of plankton flows into its mouth. Then the whale's tongue squeezes out the water, leaving only the nutritious plankton.

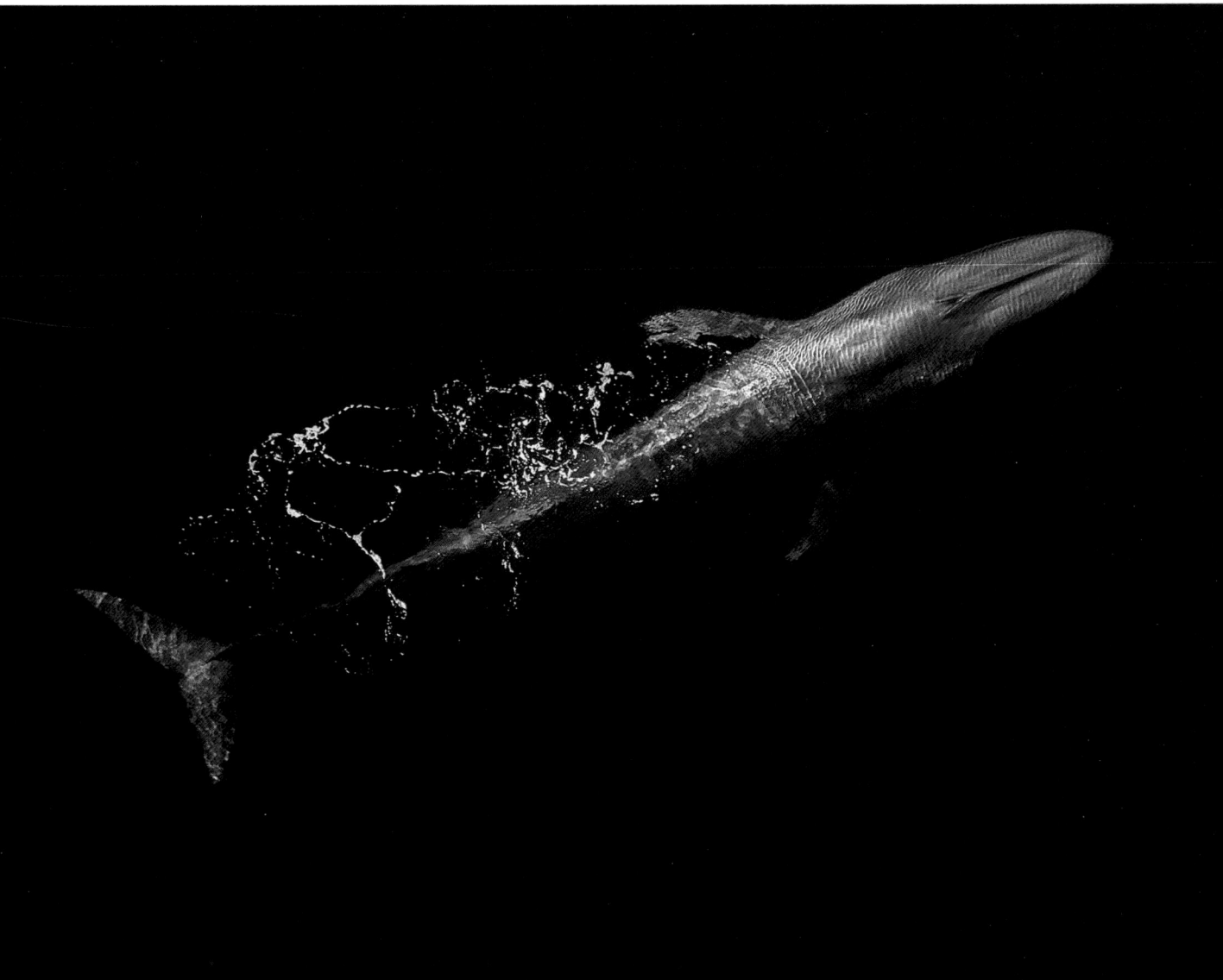

Some Baleen Whales:

Blue Whale :
Maximum length - 95 feet
Weight - 150 tons (300,000 lbs.)

Characteristics: The blue whale is the largest and fastest-swimming male. It is bluish in color except for yellow on its underside caused by a coating of tiny water plants. It is found in all oceans.

Finback Whale:
Maximum length - 82 feet
Weight - 100 tons (200,000 lbs.)

Characteristics: The finback whale has a prominent fin on its back and a slender body. It has a gray-black back, a white underside, and a white patch on the front of its right upper jaw. It is found in all oceans.

Sei Whale:
Maximum length - 55 feet
Weight - 40 tons (80,000 lbs.)

Characteristics: The sei whale looks very similar to a finback whale, but it has no white patch on its jaw. Like the finback whale, it also has a prominent fin on its back. The sei whale has a dark back and a light underside. The sei whale is found in all oceans.

Humpback Whale:

Maximum length - 50 feet
Weight - 45 tons (90,000 lbs.)

Characteristics: The humpback whale gets its name from a humped roll of fat on its back. The humpback whale has many *barnacles* and *crustaceans* on its body. It has large flippers, 12-13 feet long, used for navigation. The humpback whale is dark in color with white patches on its underside. It is found in all oceans.

Gray Whale:

Maximum length - 60 feet
Weight - 40 tons (80,000 lbs.)

Characteristics: The gray whale has a low ridge on its back in place of a fin. It is dark gray or black with many white spots and barnacles on its head. The gray whale is found in the north Pacific region.

Right Whale:
Maximum length - 60 feet
Weight - 50 tons (100,000 lbs.)

Characteristics: The right whale has a "horny" bonnet on its snout and a very large head. It has short, broad flippers. The right whale is black. It may be found in all oceans.

Bowhead Whale:
Maximum length - 55 feet
Weight - 45 tons (90,000 lbs.)

Characteristics: The bowhead whale looks very much like a right whale but it does not have a bonnet on its snout. The bowhead whale is black and is found in the Arctic.

Index

The words below also appeared in the text in *italicized* type. The page number on which each word first appeared is listed before each definition. After reading the definition, you may wish to turn back to the text page and review the new word within a sentence.

Adapted: (Page 29) Having adjusted or conformed to changing conditions.

Artiodactyls: (Page 30) A group of land mammals (antelope, caribou, pig, moose, for example) living today.

Barnacles: (Page 44) Various small marine animals that form a hard shell and cling to underwater surfaces.

Blubber: (Page 14) The term for a whale's fat.

Condenses: (Page 23) Becomes a liquid.

Crustaceans: (Page 44) Aquatic animals that have no bones or skeleton, but a shell and two pairs of antenna.

Estuaries: (Page 27) Bays where ocean salt water flows into fresh water.

Extinction: (Page 27) The condition of no longer existing as a species.

Flippers: (Page 11) The "arms" of the whale, used for turning.

Flukes: (Page 17) The tail fins of a whale, used for swimming.

Mammals: (Page 5) Animals that have spinal cords and nurse their young with milk.

Mesonychids: (Page 27) A group of mammals that appeared early in history.

Origins: (Page 27) The beginning points.

Plankton: (Page 40) Very tiny organisms that drift in the ocean.

Suffocate: (Page 21) To die from lack of air.

Parent/Child Interaction Questions

Parents: *These are questions you may ask your children in order to get them to think about whales as viable occupants of a niche in the food chain. Encourage them to explain their feelings about whales, and to ask their own questions. Clarify any misunderstandings they may have about the predator/prey relationship as it relates to whales, and explain the need to have both kinds of animals in the world. In this way, you can help foster future generations of environmentally aware and appreciative adults.*

1. The whale is the largest animal that ever lived. Does this mean that it is safe from all natural enemies?

2. You know that whales are mammals. Name some characteristics of mammals.

3. Whales live in family groups. Why do you think this is good for the whales?

4. We know that mother whales, like human mothers, hug their babies. What other things do you think whales do that humans do?

5. Do you think it would be fun to be a whale? Why, or why not?

Having your children think about and answer these questions will help them develop a healthy curiosity about other earth creatures, and to understand the importance of *all* creatures to Earth's existence as a healthy planet. Encourage children to ask their own questions. More in-depth information about whales is available in the adult NorthWord title *With The Whales.*

At more than 2 million years old,
Lake Tahoe is an ancient lake.

Natural Wonders

In California the giant **sequoia** trees amaze people. Kings Canyon National Park is home to one of the world's biggest trees. Nicknamed "General Sherman," the tree is about 275 feet (84 m) tall. It measures 25 feet (8 m) around and is more than 2,000 years old.

The hot springs and **geysers** in Wyoming's Yellowstone Park put on a great show. The famous geyser Old Faithful shoots high into the air almost every hour.

When Old Faithful erupts, the water shoots around 140 feet (42 m) into the air.

sequoia: a giant evergreen tree that grows mainly in California

geyser: an underground spring that shoots hot water and steam through a hole in the ground

In Hawaii volcanoes formed the islands. Five of Hawaii's volcanoes are still active. They are Kilauea, Mauna Loa, Hualalai, Haleakala, and Lo'ihi. Mauna Loa's last eruption was in 1984. But Kilauea has been erupting ever since 1983! Both volcanoes are part of Volcanoes National Park.

Earthquakes

Earthquakes happen when the plates that form Earth's crust shift. When the plates move, they form **fault** lines. The West is the site of several of the world's largest faults. They include the San Andreas and Hayward Faults in California and the Denali Fault System in Alaska.

Several major earthquakes have hit the region. In 1906 San Francisco, California, was heavily damaged by an earthquake and the fires that followed. About 3,000 people died. Another major earthquake hit the San Francisco area in 1989. It killed 63 people and caused $6 billion in damage.

The world's second-largest earthquake hit the Prince William Sound area in Alaska in 1964. The earthquake and the **tsunami** that followed it killed 131 people. It also destroyed much of the city of Anchorage.

fault: a crack in the earth where two plates meet; earthquakes often occur along faults

tsunami: a large, destructive wave caused by an underwater earthquake

Chapter 3

Jobs and Economy

Westerners use their region's natural resources to produce goods. Airplanes and highways move people and products in and out of the West.

Fishing, Logging, and Mining

Rivers flowing into the Pacific Ocean provide food and jobs, just as they did for the region's earliest people. Many fishers live near rivers, such as Alaska's Copper River and California's Sacramento River. Fishers catch salmon and crab in Alaska's icy waters. They fish for sardines and swordfish off the California coast and yellowfin tuna in Hawaii.

Some cities such as Seattle began as logging communities. Forests grow from Montana and Idaho down to Colorado. The northern Pacific coast has many forests too. Loggers cut down trees and plant seeds for new trees. Sawmills cut and sand the trees into boards used in construction all over the world.

The California Gold Rush lasted only a few years. But people still mine for gold and other minerals in the West. Mining companies in Alaska and California drill for oil. Tanker ships filled with oil travel from ports in Alaska and California to places all over the world.

Fishing for salmon is one of Alaska's most important industries.

Farming and Ranching

Western farmers grow many crops. More than half of the fruits, nuts, and vegetables Americans eat come from California. In Hawaii farmers grow pineapples and coffee beans. Washington orchards produce cherries, apples, and pears.

Some western states, such as Montana, have more cows than people. Cattle are raised for their meat and milk. California is the top U.S. producer of milk and other dairy products. Ranchers in Nevada and the rest of the Great Basin grow fields of hay for animal feed.

Manufacturing and Technology

Most jobs in the West don't depend on the weather or landscape. Factories build airplanes, computers, electronics, and software. Hundreds of computer companies are located in an area of northern California called the Silicon Valley. Engineers and coders design software, video games, and websites.

With more than 28,000 farms and ranches, agriculture is Montana's leading industry.

Palo Alto, California, has been a technology center since Stanford University was founded there in 1885. Stanford graduates started computer companies, such as Google and Yahoo. The social media company Facebook has its headquarters in nearby Menlo Park.

Golden Gate Bridge

The famous Golden Gate Bridge greets visitors to San Francisco, California. It was completed in 1937 to connect San Francisco and Marin County. Cables hold the 4,200-foot (1,280-m) orange steel bridge above the water.

Each day more than 100,000 vehicles cross the bridge. The bridge also has an area for people to cross on foot or by bike.

Chapter 4

PEOPLE AND CULTURE

Jobs aren't the only reason people move west. The region's climate and landscape attract new residents. People in Denver, Colorado, enjoy skiing, hiking, and mountain biking in the Rocky Mountains. In Alaska helicopters take daring skiers even higher into the mountains. In Sandpoint, Idaho, chairlifts carry people and bikes up Schweitzer Mountain. Bikers then speed down the mountain trails.

City Life

Los Angeles, California, has the largest population in the West. With 3.9 million people, it is the second largest U.S. city. Only New York City is larger. Los Angeles is the center of the American film and TV industry.

The Rocky Mountains have helped make Colorado a popular place to ski.

Westerners also enjoy nature inside their cities. Thousands of acres of parks fill Denver, Colorado, with fountains, lakes, and a zoo. Inside Portland, Oregon, trails wind through a forest. The Wilbur D. May Arboretum in Reno, Nevada, has more than 4,000 desert plants. Visitors to the Oregon Coast Aquarium in Newport watch sea lions, sea otters, seals, and other wildlife.

Many western cities are also known for their local food. People have gathered at Pike Place Market in Seattle to buy fish, herbs, and vegetables since 1907. Fresh berries, greens, and cheese are available at California's Santa Monica Farmers' Market.

Preserving Heritage

As people walk through Seattle's Pioneer Square, a huge **totem pole** reminds them of people who once lived there. American Indians carved and painted human and animal faces out of cedar to tell stories. The Totem Heritage Center in Ketchikan, Alaska, has totem poles that are more than 100 years old.

White **adobe** buildings with red clay roofs signal that much of the West was once Spanish territory. Towns such as Santa Barbara, California, preserve mission buildings built more than 250 years ago. Today California has the largest Latino population of any state. About 15 million Latinos live there.

totem pole: a wooden pole carved and painted with animals, plants, and other objects that represent an American Indian tribe or family

adobe: bricks made of clay and straw that are dried in the sun

American Indians carved totem poles to record important events or family history. Sometimes totem poles were made for a specific family member.

Green-tiled roofs topped with gold dragons mark an entrance to San Francisco's Chinatown. It's the largest Chinese community outside of China. Chinese **immigrants** came to the region during the 1800s. Many business signs are written in Chinese. In an open square, people practice martial arts and play Chinese chess.

Immigrants brought their native foods with them. People slurp Chinese noodles and eat corn tortillas everywhere from Los Angeles to Honolulu. People also enjoy American Indian foods, such as fry bread and buffalo steak. In the Northwest meals include salmon and crab from nearby waters as well.

immigrant: a person who moves from one country to live permanently in another

Celebrating the West

Westerners gather to celebrate during all seasons. Each spring in Wenatchee, Washington, they twist colorful ribbons around maypoles during the Apple Blossom Festival. Summer is for tasting garlic-flavored ice cream at the Gilroy Garlic Festival in California. Visitors to the pumpkin festival in Half Moon Bay, California, eat pies and watch people carve enormous pumpkins. Daring people jump into icy water during the Winter Carnival in Whitefish, Montana.

The West is rich not only in landscapes, but also cultures. Each year 250,000 visitors gather in Seattle, Washington, to celebrate these cultures at the Northwest Folklife Festival. Dancers move to drum beats at American Indian celebrations called powwows in every western state.

FACT

The Space Needle was built for the 1962 World's Fair in Seattle. Elevators take visitors up the 605-foot (185-m) tower to look down at the city.

At the Half Moon Bay Pumpkin Festival, people show off their pumpkin-carving skills.

With its natural beauty, outdoor activities, and job opportunities, the West has long been a place where people want to visit and live. Its growth is expected to continue for years to come.

GLOSSARY

adobe (uh-DOH-bee)—bricks made of clay and straw that are dried in the sun

fault (FAWLT)—a crack in the earth where two plates meet; earthquakes often occur along faults

geyser (GYE-zur)—an underground spring that shoots hot water and steam through a hole in the ground

glacier (GLAY-shur)—a large, slow-moving sheet of ice

immigrant (IM-uh-gruhnt)—a person who moves from one country to live permanently in another

mission (MISH-uhn)—a church or settlement where religious leaders live and work

plains (PLAYNZ)—a large, flat area of land with few trees

sequoia (suh-KWOI-uh)—a giant evergreen tree that grows mainly in California

totem pole (TOH-tuhm POLE)—a wooden pole carved and painted with animals, plants, and other objects that represent an American Indian tribe or family

tsunami (tsoo-NAH-mee)—a large, destructive wave caused by an underwater earthquake

READ MORE

Harvey, Dan. *Rocky Mountain: Colorado, Utah, Wyoming.*
Let's Explore the States. Broomall, Pa.: Mason Crest, 2015.

Levy, Janey. *Native Peoples of the Northwest Coast.* Native Peoples
of North America. New York: Gareth Stevens Publishing, 2017.

Rau, Dana Meachen. *The West.* A True Book. New York:
Children's Press, 2012.

Walker, Robert. *What's in the West?* All around the U.S. New
York: Crabtree Publishing Company, 2012.

INTERNET SITES

FactHound offers a safe, fun way to find Internet sites related to this
book. All of the sites on FactHound have been researched by our staff.

Here's all you do:

Visit www.facthound.com

Type in this code: 9781515724414

Super-cool stuff! Check out projects, games and lots more at
www.capstonekids.com

INDEX